T0146572

THIRTY 3

The light of this soldier's journey

BOBBY L. TEELE JR.

WESTBOW
P R E S S®
A DIVISION OF THOMAS NELSON
& ZONDERVAN

WestBow Press books may be ordered through booksellers or by contacting:

WestBow Press
A Division of Thomas Nelson & Zondervan
1663 Liberty Drive
Bloomington, IN 47403
www.westbowpress.com
1 (866) 928-1240

Because of the dynamic nature of the Internet, any web addresses or
links contained in this book may have changed since publication and
may no longer be valid. The views expressed in this work are solely those
of the author and do not necessarily reflect the views of the publisher,
and the publisher hereby disclaims any responsibility for them.

Any people depicted in stock imagery provided by Thinkstock are models,
and such images are being used for illustrative purposes only.
Certain stock imagery © Thinkstock.

ISBN: 978-1-5127-4198-8 (sc)
ISBN: 978-1-5127-4197-1 (e)

Library of Congress Control Number: 2016907619

Print information available on the last page.

WestBow Press rev. date: 05/06/2016

CONTENTS

Good morning, Father; I begin with praising thee,
For you alone are worthy, my Lord.
My God, thank you for your love and
life, this grace and peace
Because here and now, inside of my heart of hearts,
I understand that no man can live without your
love that protects and guides us today.
Today, as we are all daily being called to die to self for the
righteous one, who is both our King and Lord, I thrive.
And within the balance of love, I speak truth,
Realizing that the transposition must occur.
I only pray that the following prepares us for
the work that is to come ahead of us.
Because within my few years upon this earth, Father,
I have seen many people, my Lord, hurt by tragedy.
Abba, they have been blinded and left without hope
From the many trials of living these realities.
Day by day, we battle against the beast.
Sins—evermore entrapments of the flesh, and yet still,
Nonetheless, you are truth, a complete purity.
All in all, Father, you are the reason for my heart.

I trust that soon, all will be made known for me, being
seen through the eyes of life, light's endless blessings.
I start to embrace the lamp unto my feet as I
move upon this path that I must take.
It is the story of Bobby Lee's faith.
So then, here and now, I place into words my inner light.
It's a process that is a life's journey, but one that I am so
honored to have been chosen to become one with.
Thus here we all are, a believer's journal
Found written inside of the school for the
wise in heart as well as the chastened!
Your children—and Father God, in complete honesty,
I had always longed for your knowledge,
And as well, this feeling of a determination to drive.
I became determined to see your eternal glory.
Looking back, as a young child, I somehow always
felt that there was so much more to our story.
And perhaps overwhelmed is not the word
suitable enough for my initial emotion.
But as human as I am, I can't possibly
think of one more fitting.
After all, you are my Lord God.
Abba, Father, you alone created the heavens.
You spoke life, and now this world has its history—
A nation of truth that's being uncovered by your hand.
In a land of lies, who else is like the Lord, my God?

And yet your love is forever; it remains

unfailing, withstanding the test of time.

You are my inspiration, Father, when all else fails.

You're that door to be opened when change

comes and announces himself.

I realize now that nothing will ever be the same.

And in theory, we run after these so called-truths of men

When in fact, the light shines for all each and every day.

And that light is one in the same your Son,

The first of many brothers and sisters, after all.

We are all followers of the way.

To You, from Me

In the beginning, we lived, but love was
nothing more than just a word.
So life began to pull us all into opposite directions.
Time started to show his hand, and truth had allowed
the toiling away of the many insignificant pieces.
As this world had seen fit, eventually, very
little remained of our existence.
But then, suddenly, our hearts began to speak.
Years passed, and thoughts of a world being filled
with tranquility started to fade away, but slowly!
Soon the love of all loves had blessed us with his light.
So in the pursuit of truth, we had all
wandered different paths,
All in hopes of meeting after this world had its crack at us.
I began to be tossed about until I had been
captured in a whirlwind of endless thoughts.
As I would often wonder, my Lord, *What could have
ever become of those fearless teens of yesterday?*
Not to mention the heart that we had,

That inner drive and determination,
that fight to never give up
No matter what the odds may have said,
Because we are, after all, a chosen of a chosen
And yet still so willing to withstand the
very hands of time if need be,
Because that had been what the battle had commanded,
although the drama appears to be an everyday thing.
We all try and remain optimistic, not allowing the
negative vibes to push us into a depressive state;
But still, the truth needs to be spoken, and the truth is
that we are all being blindsided by the media's take
In its hot pursuit of man and his self-alienation.
I tried to regroup behind the walls of self-preservation,
And wouldn't you know it,
I heard in the news today the same message about pain.
Father God, so many people across
this globe are afraid to love,
And they do all in their power to escape the unknown.
So many war cries are constantly being
televised right before our eyes.
Therefore, Abba, I must ask this question: what of change?
Your Son has risen, our Lord Christ Jesus,
And yet families continue to walk these streets in fear,
Concealing their inner love, one of our
most powerful gifts to be given.

As a society, we at times avoid any sort of
eye contact with our fellow man.
So I wonder, my Lord, am I alone when I think that
our Father is in complete control and nothing or no
one can separate him or his love from his children?
Or could this world have it all wrong?
Besides, nothing can ever go as planned, anyway—
not unless a lot of faith, hard work, and dedication
become the constant echo within deep meditation.
I begin placing my all into this realization that you are love.
Some skeptics have tried in the past to add that this can
only be the result of a dreamer's success, perhaps.
But the evidence is forever seen in
reaching each goal for every step,
Because in the end of all, only one
knows the outcome of our lives.
But still, we all continue with our
quarrels and endless bickering—
Arguments over a whole lot of nothing as
we remain blinded to the facts.
So now in humility, I ask what to do
When all that we have is a history of
misuse from me unto you.
I mean, after all, I write as slave to your poetry's claim.
This is my journal, a gift given to you
as a dedication from me,
Because all that I have is this, this story of one.

I'm just a voice crying out from the wilderness of
this world, trying my best to come to grips with all
that you have shown me in your holy Word,
Because these are hard times, and with their
confusion, they try their best to pollute our vision
And corrupt our recollection. It is a very sick and
twisted game that they all play, if you ask me,
After our spirits and minds!
But consistently, I strive forward, Abba, toward hope and
vision as I begin to embrace and accept my mission.
I'm trying to do all that I possibly can now
to scrap together all that's left.
After all, we need some sort of
substance to sustain ourselves.
Father, this is just a letter from me on behalf of your people
In this land in such desperate need of your love.
We all pray for your heavenly light to
return and ignite us, Abba,
In hopes that the peace that surpasses all
understanding will abide forever in us,
A people of a people who are so much
in need of their Messiah.
These are in fact very heartfelt words,
Father, a cry for forgiveness.

A Better Focus—My Story

Well, my story is a soldier's journey, but it's a
journey toward the top, Mount Zion.
Where we started, no one could have imagined that
life would thrive in Orlando's inner-city projects!
But here we all are, a family determined to
live the promise of peace and love,
And at times I reflect, and I can see
how easy it was to give in.
Back in those days, I had a constant
thought of calling it quits—
Just another statistic following the crowd upon
a path of self-defeat and self-torment.
I really can't say what it was; I just know how I felt—
A bunch of mixed emotions, frustration,
and bitter attitudes toward people.
I can never forget how poverty's hand stayed on
the eyes and minds of the inner-city struggles.
Being seen through my eyes, I can recall,
Father, that day in front of the mirror.
Face-to-face with myself, I had come to a place within me,

A point where I realized that I can't
change the many ways of man.
But I had a choice, a voice,
A right to choose to live and love! Or I could have
been blinded by the many stereotypes of society,
Becoming one of many being emotionally fed,
Those who feel almost as if they've been forsaken,
forever walking in the shadows of disgrace.
And I have learned, Abba, that when we are on
that side of life, we begin the forsaking,
Overlooking the very love you continue
to give us each and every day.
So often, I had felt almost as if I had
been plagued by my past
With all the constant reminders of going back and forth
with myself: *Will I change?* or *Why won't I accept this grace?*
Because it was all on me, day in and day out—
Not to mention the giant sin cloud that seemed to be
forever hovering around us while we were out and about.
For reasons unknown, I felt hurt, just
because, and discouraged,
Discouraged with the drastic turn in music,
Because all of their raps had become about
money and drugs, drugs and guns.
But these same things aid in the
destruction of our communities,
Leading us all down a path of darkness and eventually
putting an end to our world as we know it!

Besides, a lot of people are still stuck, not
knowing if they can ever find a way out,
Lost to the many misconceptions about
others' fabricated lifestyles.
These open eyes allow it to be so that we all can see.
It was a false hope, thinking that this world had
ever cared about any one of our souls.
Also through living, I can now see. It is hard, at
times, trying to salvage hope from within the
ash heaps of the lost and the forgotten.
After all, some sheep are still missing,
With so many childhood friendships forever lost,
without any hope of ever Facebooking them—
Truth be told, all that seems to be left for
them are honorable mentions,
As if they were the soldiers who had fallen in battle,
Into the depths of the trenches. But as it
is with everything else, Father,
Life goes on, and time moves forward.
I then began to notice the many challenges
that started to be placed before me.
My eyes had been opened, and I started to question
things like what this world really had to offer me.
Then suddenly, your spirit, Abba, had led me into focus.
I began anew! Thus my thoughts had changed,
and I had adopted a new outlook on life, like
How can I impact this world on a positive note
So that those after me can study?

Because only you know the return date, Father, and
whether they would truly motivate themselves, Abba.
I'm speaking of their inner beings, because at the end of all
my discoveries, maybe my small piece could have helped
someone else move forward with this grand puzzle.
In the place and time of the redeemed,
predestined, and determined,
I, young Bobby, continue in my search
to find my truth and purpose,
For since I can remember, I only wanted all of
creation to have the same focus as I do,
And that shall forever remain heaven,
Because in doing so, I truly do believe that we all would
please the Lord God, the Supreme Being, Christ Jesus,
The one who is our very hope and Redeemer and
our sanctification, because without the love of
God, all our souls would have remained cold.
So, yes, the obvious is now made known. Without
the truth, my eyes would have remained closed.
My heart could not have ever expressed this love.
And every man, woman, and child
truly would have been lost,
Destined for lives in the abyss, a hopeless walk
in eternal darkness. So I thank you again,
Abba, for welcoming me into your family.

My Heart

In order for me to be here, speaking of love,
I at first had to discover my heart.
Thus I had to journey and find the inner me.
So for now, let's just call him young Bobby,
A soldier with a free spirit, a soul,
Destined to find peace—and now the eyes
of my heart have been opened.
I thank you, Abba, because the dreams of today
have become my passions of tomorrow.
Even when the skies are gray and the past tries to
run rampant, appearing to be untamed, I love!
Because in truth, I have discovered the
one, he who is all that I need.
Therefore, unto the one who guides me,
I believe and trust in him—
The Lord God's Holy Spirit.
I'm now realizing I can no longer look at fear as
though it were my familiar surrounding,
Because God has delivered me from me.
The old man is long gone and forgotten.

It's only us now, the unified front of faith,
A family that looks beyond the surfaces
of earthly possessions,
Brothers and sisters that are forever filled with the
love and life of the Lord God's Holy Spirit
As we all become showered evermore
in our Father's grace and mercy.
May his light of eternity shine from within every heart
forever and ever more—and it is because of this fact.
We are a body of believers that is not afraid to shout it!
Upon each and every continent, may all
of this earth know and trust.
There is a God, and Lord Jesus was and still is to come.
He's alive here and now, inside you and me,
A chosen of a chosen, trusting in our Father's
words when he said, "God sent in Godspeed."
Above and beyond the laws that govern the flesh,
we continue upon this soldier's journey.
A journey some critics may question and ask—but is it
not a journey into the unknown, into a distant land?
But I say in one word when asked, *heaven,*
Because it is the paradise reserved for
your loved ones and the faithful.
My Lord is King Jesus, and your life, my Lord, is so
precious. Yet today so many in the world, I fear, will
grow without ever knowing of your sacrifice and love.

Your light is a story nowadays that
so often goes as one untold
But seemingly ever so present, with so
many of this world's researchers.
One would think that they would just
look at all of the evidence:
The truth of creation, the many animals, our souls.
And who can ever forget about the
first as well as second heavens
When their lights alone inspire both young
and the old to dream the impossible?
Even though we still war against all
that protects and guides us,
These words are spoken unto the chosen—
An inspiration to seek out and find a focus,
A focus for one's inner growth, a development within mind.
But as a people, we're all walking around
today as if we're zombies on fright night
When there's so much constantly to face
Just with the everyday things of life in this world.
We are the very people, the same ones who continue
to pile up more and more of the garbage.
I wonder, Abba—when will we grow tired
of all the nonsense and face the facts?
Without our King, we are all lost and without a Savior.
Where can the weary tarry in search of their rest?

I suppose we don't know love when it's
standing right in front of us.
But as soon as our hearts are broken, we can recognize
exactly where the real love had been all along.
It's kind of funny how we want things so badly—
So much so that we then pray for them as
well as the strength to accept all.
But never do we just stop and really
listen to the words of our hearts.
My Lord, I pray that we all can get it
right as well as trust in you,
Your holy Word, before all is truly too late. Truth!

Poetic

The silence—I can hear the ocean, Abba,
as I await the beautiful dawn!
I receive a message; these open reflections
are, after all, blessings upon blessings.
And through self-awareness,
I embrace this challenge
Because of you and your light, my Lord.
Forever gracing us all with your presence, I can see!
Thy Rose of Sharon—no matter what, teaching us to
become fishermen of men, seeing one's inner essence.
And without the stress of doubt or the veil of self-neglect,
I rise this day, only to be greeted by thy bright Morning Star.
And I had waited last night for the love of life.
And in question was that very
harmonious attitude I once had
When at first I was drawn to your love.
Once before, I had been afraid to
travel this road in first light,
So often distracted in my past, and now a deep thought.
Well, after all, it had run first leg in the race—

That is, until a new emotion had arrived!
I had an assumption, Abba, that I could never
be as free as I had once dreamt—at least not
how I had envisioned before December!
And yet my heart remains a reflection of hope's promise.
But emotions, these emotions continue to
mislead me toward self-destruction,
As I have often thought, *If only life would push me into new*
Jerusalem, perhaps then all would not seem so bad for me.
And I wouldn't have these same feelings of doubt or that
oh-so-depressive attitude toward living everyday life.
You know it—that "me against the world"
mentality that continues to stride,
Deep down, trying its best to withdraw the very
deposit that you've placed within, inside of me.
But, my Lord Jesus, only you know if this is
all one with the master plan for me.
My life, Teele—
A daydreamer of sorts,
A man on a mission to complete, to put the past behind me,
All of the failures and loss—
I begin to become, more and more today, alive!

Believing & Conceiving

For years now, I have dared to be different.
But above all, I long to be freed!
You see, I had been delivered into this
world, a man before the child.
But I couldn't become him, because
I wouldn't let go of the wild,
My past—
A fleshy person drawn to all things that get their
meaning and reasoning out of this world.
But my destiny was to break free, leaving
behind the shackles of a depraved mind.
It is because of a life force like none other I can speak now.
Because what is mine is yours, and as well,
your spirit resides forever in me.
Love and life! A life in love—people, it's just a small
sacrifice to pay to see God's love face to face.
Besides, I am the same one who used to think that
nothing inside of the hearts of men is destined to love.
As well, nothing or anyone could generate a
truth from within but here and now.

I must confess, Abba Father,
I have found everlastingly all that's needed for
success inside the light of our Lord Christ Jesus.
I'm realizing now, dreams are not the doorways to
heaven, and everyday life is not the battlefield of regret.
Heartache and determination
Love truth; life is what you make out of it,
and one must always remember.
From the smallest of the small to the biggest of the large,
We all have our parts, roles to play in this
wonderful thing that we all call life,
Continuing in the promise upon this mission to strive.
But one must also remember that wisdom is found in truth,
And only one can hold the claim to all as well
as wear the crown of righteousness.
As I often pray, Abba Father, who art in heaven,
Hollowed be thy name, and may the
love of life always abide in me
And grace walk before us in this land of shame.
My King, please guide and protect your loved
ones, the dedicated and changed.
My God, it is because of you that now, in the name of Jesus,
I can turn this present-day page of life without fear.
I'm focused, determined now, and also more devoted than
I have ever been in my entire life before this moment.
Father, you are my all, the Lord Christ Jesus,
The truth and resolution to this world's confusion.

And unto the Prince of Peace, you are
forever, and everlasting is your reign.
As holy and true you will always remain,
you're my completion, Abba.
I trust in your Word. So then no matter what
the next hour may or may not bring,
I realize I must trust in you,
Because life is to love, and to love is to live life in its
fullest for each day that we are blessed to live.
Thus I begin to cherish every moment and praise the only
one who is capable of giving all people such a great gift.
As I now realize how blessed I am to even be
breathing the very life that is needed inside of me
So that I may have this will to carry on—
My God, just to think.
If not for you and your love, where would
this journey have taken us,
With so many dreams shattered before us and
even more people lost to their bad habits?
But by your hand and through the power of your Word,
I can see the light that changes all and
places everything into perspective.
King of the Hebrews, my Lord!
You're both Alpha and Omega, Father.
And I haven't forgotten, Abba; you alone
showed me the gate to access all. That has
never been obtained by my hands before.

And yes, Lord, your will be done, not mine.

Because a love like yours, what man

or woman can ever fathom

Your love and grace, my majesty? Believing

is conceiving the fifth day.

Daydreamer

Today, a daydreamer had begun to drift,
Drifting in and out of this world.
At one point, I was distant from all,
on an island all by myself.
Here and now, though, I am focused upon the goal.
So then no longer can I place my faith in man, nor
can I allow myself to be turned about by my past.
Because a life being lived then was truly
no life being lived at all, Father.
But I am now realizing that hope is pure and honest.
So if I claim to have hope but lack faith, then
to whom can I be encouragement?
(Selah) My emotions—well, my
emotions can be wrong at times
And so steer me into a complete opposite direction,
One in which I shouldn't be heading anyway,
perhaps on the other side of the fence,
In a situation where I may not have
any business in the first place.
In other words, I prefer to remain open-minded,

Focused upon the positive rather than a negative.
I'm beginning to see life as a blessing more so now,
Rather than a constant battleground for testing.
I start reminding myself of your
everlasting lessons, Father—
The love and truth, the honor and dedication.
So then, mirror me back
As I close my eyes and soon awaken in a land
of spirit and truth, peace and love.
A deep thought—once I was lost in my other
life, but now I am found in God.
A light of truth, a promise to love,
As well as the voice that speaks correction
above the static of this world's chaos—
I do believe that this is my turning point,
Awakening unto truth, realizing who I am inside you.
These moments are indeed priceless, and so I pray, Abba.
I pray that all embrace this light of eternity,
For I trust that I have seen the love of God.
And in believing so, there can never be a greater love.
Therefore, my Lord, if I am truly asleep,
than please, my Master,
Allow my slumber to remain for just a little while longer.
Because I can see the coming abroad; dreams seek
a reality as the past is remembered no more.
Thus, now I open my eyes and look into the sky
As I begin to envision the storm clouds gathering.

But regardless of whatever, I shall not fret,
Because you are my shelter, my God.
You are the strength needed to overcome life's
many obstacles and man's countless spectacles.
After all, my Lord, you're the great I Am.
You are the truth before all is seen.
I run toward your light, Father, praying
for each and every soul to be saved,
Because the battle is being fought, but
the war has already been won.
So nonetheless, I write the very life
that you've blessed me with—
The daydreamer's truth, your soldier's journey: day six!

Today

I awoke this morning feeling revived as well
as assured within the promise of life.
I'm thankful, my Lord—truly thankful for this time.
As I embrace your love, Father—a
lasting impression, Abba—
At last, I am finally surpassing life's
cycle of a hounding depression,
Arriving in the state where months become
days and days become months
And what once was no longer holds value anymore.
I hear that life's a constant, endless bout
that is said to help build character.
But some would beg to differ and much rather
avoid the entire process of being challenged.
Because I can recall a man who did whatever
he could to separate himself from all he
had ever come into contact with.
He began embracing the notion of becoming
one of the many lost and forgotten.
His heart became cold and didn't beat, at least not properly.

You see, grief had captured his soul, as he would often say.

Love had chosen to leave him alone.

Therefore to him, love didn't have a voice.

Darkness had begun its work in becoming his abode.

But hope's fight is an endless light. Your light, Father—

It shines even in the darkest of dark,

Seen in and through the deepest of deep,

Felt even in the latest of the night and time, Abba.

Time has no control over your power—so yes, even

this man had to bear witness to your truth,

First by humbling himself as well as bringing all

of his burdens at the foot of your throne.

And also, he had to come to grips with all

The goodness of your love, the unfailing

grace that's you, Abba.

In the order of Melchizedek is forever

King Jesus our high priest,

Interceding on behalf of the sinner—

One of the many gifts of your grace that

we are all so unworthy to receive

And yet you continue to give as a blessing.

And as life continues on, I am learning, Father.

I am learning that we as a people so often think that

our situations are either so great or so small that

you wouldn't trouble yourself with them or us.

But as I am blessed to grow,

Maturing inside of this molding,

The shaping in the likeness and character of your Son,
Abba, I become more aware of the schemes of the enemy,
The mass of confusion that floats about
in the evening as the sun sets.
As well, many lies are told in the early
morning as the birds begin singing
By way of the troubled soul, a sneak
peek into the troubled man.
Even so, Father, I had cried out on behalf of this man, Abba,
Praying that your hand touch him in his life
in the many ways that only you can,
Because I can still remember those mountains
and how they moved once you spoke
As well those deep valleys—but even
more so, your gentle touch
And how it reminded us of your presence in the face of
adversity when opposition stood against your chosen.
But nevertheless, no matter how high
or the depths of any sea,
Your Word remains eternal. It's
steadfast and forever complete.
Therefore, I am convinced
Nothing can stop the Lord God from delivering his people.
So then, I am now encouraged by the
very seed that you've planted.
My spirit, Abba—e longs to produce
a good work for you, Father,

A fruit that is pure and capable of sharing with all.
And because I trust in you, my King, and
shall become this soldier of your love,
I believe in this moment, the day of my Lord's grace.
I begin exploring, Father, the countless ways that I can
allow myself to do and become one with your love.
I start viewing myself differently than I had before now.
I see so much more; I am a tool
Ready to be used by you.
I realize now that so many people live today without light.
They only know the darkness that they've been
exposed to, so they mimic what they see.
And since you alone know if tomorrow will ever come,
I pray that our present presents a reasoning
within its much-needed change,
Because the grass continues to grow and rivers flow.
So I believe that each day has within itself
a purpose behind every miracle,
A message of hope. Dreams can come true when
we dream the impossible inside of you.
My King Jesus, it is you!
Because everything is everything because of you.
You're the Son who gave all to please Abba Father.
I often laugh as I cry on the inside, knowing that
your walk of faith did more in three years on
this earth than any other march in history.
And as a soldier, I can only ask to march,

To live and rise in your name, every day,
for each breath and every moment
Until the end!
This day, this present moment—
It's so much more than just another day, though.
It's a beautiful melody of countless blessings,
A reason to laugh or a much-needed
pause after tears have been shed.
Yes, a song of one today! Today I
dedicate to my King, Lord Jesus.

A Promise to Love

I speak in love's truth here and now, even when
I had found it difficult to believe, Father.
You showed me how,
How to love and grow in faith
As well as how to live a life inside of the light of freedom.
My Lord, it is because of you that I
can give my all in life today,
For every breath that I am blessed with to breathe.
And Father, your wisdom is so beyond our human
comprehension, as you've often shown me.
Sometimes this world shakes us, and as a people,
we can allow its quakes to wreck our nerves.
So we then become anxious, not knowing that
we allow ourselves to become vulnerable.
We begin to forget, forgetting all that
you have ever taught us.
In moments such as these, we start to lose heart.
Therefore, we allow this world's confusion
to misguide us all into the dark,
Into a realm of complete disarray—

A challenge, we could call it! But what about its temptation?
So often, we're blindsided with life's many
challenges of everyday tribulations.
We draw our own cords, Abba, as
foolishly we then snap the lines.
But as soon as we all begin to fall, Father,
We cry out for your hand to hold
And your arms to open,
Praying that you will save us from the
flames of the fire. My God!
At times, I had foolishly taken for granted the
everlasting goodness of your unfailing love.
It's a mistake I wish could be taken away.
But it is a lesson, I feel, well learned.
Day by day, I had been struggling within,
Avoiding all contact with the Spirit man,
Daily just battling against self,
Giving in to the temptations of the flesh.
It had become a constant roller coaster for
me, appearing to never have an end.
But, my Lord, because you are love,
I had trusted in you.
And by your grace, I have been spared,
Taken away from my manmade mental prison.
And just to think—I had once been seen as confusion's fool.
And now, I try and adjust as well as adapt
to being called one of your sons.

The supreme being, creation's Creator, I
have but this one question, Father.
Why is it I have been blessed to have made it this far?
In knowing and now realizing I am only a mere
sinner, being saved by your unfailing grace,
Being controlled by life itself,
I bear witness to your love for each and every day.
As I observe, Abba, always after you,
I see people are changing, truly.
As some are changing for the better, and
others may need just a little more time.
But regardless, I can see your Word at work,
Still blessing your children here and now in this world.
Thus from the pages of history, the light
of the world shines evermore.
My God, you are my shelter and comforter.
As I can recall, it was a very cold winter
when I had first enlisted.
Everything in my world had been turned upside down.
As a much younger Teele, then I had become
a constant when it had come to distance.
I barely spoke to you, Father,
For I had yet to trust or call upon your love faithfully,
Not to mention identifying the facts as well as
seeking out the truth were not things I had at
the very top of my priority list at first!
Needless to say, I used to rely upon the wisdom of the world.

Them—but who were they?
The many people who had gained their knowledge
through the so-called trials and errors of life.
But, be as it may, life's song.
I would often sing of change, but I
couldn't quite pinpoint the way.
Some people had claimed to know the answers, but in
return, they only helped to cloud my judgement.
A lack of discernment truly in my earlier phase,
And yet I continued on this life,
Being blessed in the name of grace's Creator.
As my metaphor tries to speak, a visual of your light,
It's almost as if your love is like a cool
summer's breeze on a hot summer night,
My lifeline that I am always in need of,
as I stand here forever amazed,
Being faced with tests each day.
As my reality shouted out for attention,
I had begun craving deeply, Father, for your truth.
Because in my heart, I was determined for a way out—
Out of my town as well as my state.
I became out of my mind, because I had begun
to feel the many entrapments of the flesh.
As life would have it, spiritually I had felt
myself being pushed toward the edge.
Finally, I had reached my crossroads,
At a place where a choice had needed to be made.

I could either choose to live the love
that is life or turn my back
And embrace all that goes hand in
hand in this land of shame.
But all of the glory is given unto our King.
The eye in I choose your light, my God,
As well as your everlasting Word, my Lord.
Then soon after life as I once knew it started to change,
Friendships began to be tested.
And upon every front of relations, my heart
had seen your Word's testament,
The truth that you are speaking now from my innermost,
Revealing all even before the time had presented itself.
But by the mighty hand of love, I am realizing now
You'd been preparing me for life's test, my first season.
Because I believe that every road traveled will
have signs ahead, and some sort of construction
may lie uproad, detouring us—
A reroute of our time, but nonetheless,
We should view this as a tool for sharpening our minds.
Now in the spirit, I realize, all hearts are
being equipped with a message.
And I truly do look forward to this world's final summary,
A proclamation; perhaps the unification will speak.
So our next line of soldiers will have a mission statement
to command even more of this world's leaders.
After all, I am but one man,

Forever learning how to trust and believe.
Because within trusting, I can see now
what it takes to become a leader.
I work harder, training even more than I ever had before.
And within my preparation, my senses
have become heightened.
And I begin to notice that the troops in my
camp are hungry for knowledge, Abba, but I
feel even more for your Word, Father.
Yet so many weapons are being formed against us.
We motivate each other as much as
possible to remain focused,
Reminding one another of the key principles to success.
And they will forever be God the Father,
God the Son, and God the Spirit
As we all continue in prayer, seeking out
life's answers for its many trials
Within your holy Word.
Now with our eyes forever locked
upon you, as well as your Son,
We place our complete trust in the holy Trinity,
Especially with all of your many works
through the many soldiers before us,
Those whom your holy Word calls upon as the
faithful and patriarchs of spiritual freedom.
We as the children can only pray that we
will impact this world as they did,

Because the way things are looking, living
today in life appears to be so bleak
In a land and time where heartache
appears to hearken upon the weary.
The lost and downtrodden seem to go unnoticed!
At times, it's almost as if this world's
society anticipates its depletion.
Or could it be our souls are lacking in faith just a little?
Then again, perhaps I can only see through
these eyes that you've blessed me with.
Even so, I want to help.
I need that peace within mind as well as joy,
The joy that comes with the satisfaction
of reaching at least one.
After all, I am only one,
One with this message of your love.
I have this deep yearning, Abba.
I must show my brothers and sisters
that there is another route,
One that is so much greater than the
road that leads to desolation—
A way, the truth that is spoken,
The Word that saves all who believe
in it from self-destruction,
That one voice, the one voice, speaking above all the others.
We all know of the noise and the confusion
among this world's chaos!

Because truly I say, from my heart of hearts,
I believe that we as a people need to really
embrace the cure for our human doubt
And finally stop feeding upon this world's madness
And drinking from its cup of deception.
We must all proclaim that your love is
our reasoning unto life itself.
Without wavering, or any more doubt,
We have to truly rely upon your Word of revelation,
Trusting that it is the truth and it won't leave us in limbo.
Not to mention, we are a people in need of your
direction, an isolated focus upon King Jesus.
But hear me out, world: the real difference is
that the love of God is real and true.
So then, there isn't a need for a pill or any type of surgeries.
After all, this is the antidote for a life
that has been lived in fear.
Because a new life begins with our meditation
upon your holy Word, my heavenly Father.
And inside of this truth, this light, I
have discovered an open door,
A door that will lead all who enter through
it into an entirely different realm,
A blessing of everlasting portions,
A gift in the form of grace and mercy by way
of the unseen and the undiscovered.

Some may argue that this is the stuff that

dreams are made out of, but me, myself,

I can only stand in amazement,

Just thinking how blessed our hearts are, these lives we live.

And still we are all allowed to dream and

at times gaze upon such a love,

The light of all creation,

The voice that calls us out from among them,

Those who would much rather embrace the darkness.

Thank you again, a billion times over.

Thank you for allowing your love to shine in our hearts—

The eighth day of your soldier's journey.

A promise to love.

Hyssop

Father God, I began this day with a
question for my fellow comrades.
What is the truth that surpasses all human understanding?
Because the answer is rather simple for me: the great I Am,
All in all, my light to each and every
step I have ever taken this life.
My Lord really is the greatest love ever known to man,
My God, giver of heavenly peace, as well as my Lord,
King Jesus, thy majesty.
It's day nine, and I can see its reality within
the extreme inside of a troubled land.
So many of us look for our answers, Abba, but we
always search for them in all of the wrong places.
As I am learning, my Lord, this day,
Your wisdom is true power, and your love has
become the shield that protects your children
from all this world tries to throw at us.
As these seasons continue to change, I start
to view your love as a cure for all.

Day by day, your charity becomes a medication
that can be compared to none other.
That's why I like to call it my hyssop—
Because it is truth, all pure and so natural.
Your love has become this soldier's laughter
and joy throughout this life's many
reoccurring scenes of hate and sadness.
So then, I feel it's safe to say that your Word is light,
A light that stands as a living torch in our present day,
Sent to ignite this world's next generation
of leaders and survivors.
As I walk, moving toward you, I bring all food for thought
For the spiritual as well as the physical natures,
But unto all who take steps forward and beyond.
You might view this as a journeyman's song,
But now as I think about it,
I must take a pause as I start to take a step back
and really begin to observe your love.
I find myself reflecting upon each and every
comforting word that you've ever spoken to me.
But my God, I can't give an account of your
everlasting riches when asked to do so,
Because the number is truly too great.
For who can keep track of the Lord's many blessings?
And truly I say, life becomes a very special gift
upon blessings for the one who knows your
love on a much more personal level.

As I now turn my focus upon this walk
that we've all begun to take,
This love that we all call faith, that which is a race
for the heart as much so for the mind and spirit,
A life, Father, that I welcome with open
arms and truly do embrace.
But I would be lying to myself, Abba, if
I didn't tell you that at times,
I find this love hard to swallow.
The Great Physician unto my weary soul, Comforter,
Father, and my security for our leap into tomorrow—
The truth, you are all,
My here and now, healing me from the inside
out, the spirit of the Most High.
The Lord's Holy Ghost, you've counseled me,
Speaking all truth about all things
throughout my entire life.
It's no wonder why now, all I can speak of is love
In my Lord's name,
Because it is in love that I have arrived at this point.
And it is through love I shall continue to rise.
By your unfailing mercy and grace, I stand.
I am forever in debt to your wisdom.
It is a gift, that on my own, I could have never purchased,
Therefore a gift that can only be received through faith.
My King, your lessons are now one within me.

Thank you, Rabbi, for the patience
with which you've taught me,
As well as showing your seed how words
need to be accompanied by actions.
So then if a person claims to have faith, but truly doesn't,
Then his or her life will show proof as well
as the fruit that each will bear.
But as it is and shall always remain for me,
Faith is true belief and all that is desired.
Being as it is of a pure and true nature,
it can only come through one,
The Lord of lords, the supreme being,
The love of all life, the very reason why
we battle against the enemy,
Continuing to do so until the change of light
as well as the hope of today are awakened
within each and every household,
Every city and state,
Until every heart knows and trusts there lives a Savior,
The Son of the living God.
Even now, I myself battle, fighting against all that
tries to mislead all of the Father's children.
I am speaking about every evil spirit.
They only want to destroy and confuse our inner beings!
All of them are agents of the enemy,
Each one of them desiring to dim every light.
And in time, they wish to have a completely darkened word,

Both mentally as well as spiritually!
Using all that they have, they place their
target upon the body of Christ,
Longing for a day, when the world is
entirely filled with disbelief.
As I now sit here alone in the Spirit,
I ponder this thought.
Could then, in that moment, someone truly say that
the world would be possessed with lost souls?
Heaven forbid that it should ever take place—
A people within a nation walking by
fear and not Spirit, in faith,
A mindless being looking to substitute eternal
salvation for this world's so-called riches.
Therefore, we the children of the Most High, we fight.
We march on until there's no one who can say that they've
been spiritually abandoned or physically left behind.
From one end of this world to the other, we
march in the blessed name of our King,
Proclaiming his message!
Salvation is yours, freely given as a gift from
God, but only through him, his Son, can
one receive this precious gift of love.
There can only be one way to true freedom,
And that way is truth, and that truth's name is Jesus,
Both Lord of lords and King of kings,
One conquering lion of Judah, all-powerful

And forever knowing for everyone. The
Lord Jesus becomes everything,
His Spirit, my King, the one who had sacrificed all,
A love that will last forever more.
Above all things, these are some of the many
reasons why we all so desperately need our
great physician, aren't they, Abba?
Truth be told, I can honestly see it
Coming over the horizon, through the clouds.
There is hope, even now in this battle zone.
Creation speaks as I can tell some souls are being lifted.
Some I can hear through the many
messages I receive from family.
There's so much to say, and I feel so little time.
But as long as your light shines,
continuing to bless this body,
Our love shall always fuse, as our hearts
will lead us all in your way,
Doing all that you've commanded us to do.
I am praying for the day when all of the little girls
of this world will truly be able to breathe free
And can enjoy every big, blue sky,
As all of the young men grow up into upstanding citizens
whom their families and communities could be proud of,
As we all continue to reach new heights.
I still believe and trust each family that prays together

will soon realize that there is a God who answers and
blesses those who trust in him and remain faithful.
Family, to all and for every broken heart,
you should know and believe.
There is hope inside of true love.
No matter what this world may or may not say,
We are all blessed to have this opportunity at life
And also have God's grace to change.
So then I say, why not become the best
you that you can possibly be?
Because as I revisit who I was,
That person whom I once knew,
I begin to see just how lonely he was, because there
never appeared to be any hope for this world.
Men and women had all seemed to
run toward ill-gotten gain,
Trying to all reason with death in hopes
of borrowing against time,
Doing all that they had felt could be done to escape change.
I never did understand man and his crazy ways.
I had fought with this for years on end, it had seemed,
To a point where I thought that I would drive myself
mad searching for answers to our insanity.
With all of our potential that we possess as human beings,
And yet still—families, Abba! They're
being left without dads
In a survival-of-the-fittest world

With a dog-eat-dog mentality!
I often ponder this thought: what will happen when
all of this world's so-called competition is gone
and the lesser or misfortunate is no more?
I ask, Abba, will then society begin doubting itself?
Perhaps the overlooking of your love will cease,
And all of the newly open-minded people will
run toward a self-awareness in belief.
Then again, I suppose the constant wars speak
so much better in volume for man.
And just to think—we are all said to be
humane and not the animal.
Day nine—hyssop.

Life's Light

I had once dreamt a dream of all dreams, Father;
it had been a dream for all of the ages.
I dreamt that all of humanity—old
world as well this new one—
Had both come into your light of true
peace and worshipped you
In light of the times.
All men had come into this realization.
All of their selfishness was and had always been futile.
We all lived under the Son of your love
In harmony, embracing the truth that is our Lord Jesus.
Inside of this love, all of our lights had shone as one.
But like most things of today,
I had to awaken, and in doing so, the
dream then had faded away,
Which had brought me to this day.
Within this moment, a question:
When people, when all is over, then what?
Who's left, or better yet, who gets to
say who lives or perishes?

Because upon this earth, within this world,
As man and his demands continue to do their damage,
I begin to ponder the outcome of society,
Because a person only needs the eyes
to see and the ears to hear
To realize that these walls are starting to crumble down.
And for more than ten centuries, we have been at war now!
The constant threats of a world in
famine continue to taunt us
As these poor living conditions for the unfortunate
in numbers rise higher and higher,
Not to mention these endless crimes that are
being committed against our neighbors.
And now we have an issue with this
thing called global warming!
In a land of the free and home of the brave,
I have born witness to a life taking its
very first breath, and I must say,
It's a precious gift to take part in a life
being seen in such a fragile stage.
And many soldiers are being buried as their family
members all fall apart at their funerals.
I cry out, Abba! What can ever become of a people who
know of love but are so unable to express it completely
to a world that so greatly needs to be loved?
My Lord, I ask because I seek the answers to
man and all of his unformulated cancers.

Time and time again, we ignore all of the
warning signs of a coming end.
And yet, as soon as things all start to resemble
their type of hope, being refreshed and anew,
Your light of all lights shines, Father,
Exposing the many lies of men.
As your Word reveals, some only pretend
to have a love for their fellow man.
But as soon as the moment presents itself,
We as a whole, we turn right around with a price for his life
As it lies balanced within our very own hands.
It's so sad to bear witness firsthand these
results from the tests of men.
We all try so hard to convince ourselves
that our wrongs will be made right.
Just as long as we can sleep, seeing a way through the night,
We're constantly telling ourselves that all will be okay.
Tomorrow will be that day of our redemptive cry.
The only problem is that tomorrow never seems to
awaken that inner love deep down in the inside.
And as these days have progressed on,
I have observed man calling out, seeking
wisdom from Mother Nature.
As it appears, the wind often blows; the hurricane's
rains wash the chaos away at times.
But for the most part, the heat index puts us
that much closer to the judgement day

Because the humidity alone in the south is
enough to drive a sane person insane.
My Lord, I start to reflect again upon the family and
our so-called picture-perfect portraits of innocence.
I try not to cry, because my eyes have already bled the
tears of a generation in mourning, but what's next?
Father we've seen so many taken away from us.
We all begin to wonder,
Will there ever be a spiritual regeneration,
some sort of movement?
In a sense, we all seek our modern-day Moses!
We're a flock in need of a shepherd—
Our leader, willing to recommunicate
to us your commandments.
Because just the other day, Abba,
I had witnessed a race of endless threats.
People are ambushing souls,
Apparently forgetting all about your love and how
we are all supposed to give to one another.
In these communities, tragedies strike every day.
And at times, some open hearts prevail, but for what?
At least a year! Because then reality calls, and this
cold world proceeds on with its countless assaults.
Soon after, those same ol' walls of judgement and self-
righteousness—well, they get built right back up again.
Life's crazy at times, living here.
Often we walk at night, so afraid,

Almost as if there's some sort of shadow
of death upon our heels,
Out to conquer and separate us all.
But I have this message for the chosen. Listen up!
Terror came to terrorize the sensible and reasonable minds,
Those who seek a better way to love each other.
Human beings are becoming a better
species as well as a stronger people.
Because in my eyes, all who embrace hate
Welcome their own; perhaps that is why there are so
many miserable workplaces today in the world.
I can recall how I had once viewed this
reality as a black and white scene.
But now I can see the many colors of the rainbow,
And they all bleed the same pain,
Because all one has to do is change the channel
And begin to witness how sin looks to become reborn
Again and again in search of his new name.
He tries to seep in through the motion
of modern-day technology.
But nonetheless, we can all see through
his many distortions.
And yet it still hurts so bad to see so
many of us flocking to his lies.
We, in moments such as these, fall victim to uncertainty.
We begin to then willingly put on sin's dark
cloak of shame and corruption.

Father, your Word is our only strength in these times.
Who else is there, assuring us of hope's light
shining so brightly on the other side
As these so-called news reports only add
more and more fuel to our fires?
We continue ablaze!
But in the dark, Father, I ask, how can one see
another's point of view that's trying to be made
As they've begun raging a war against them in anger?
Headlines perhaps would read, "Today's
People Are Lost without a Prayer."
At least sometimes, this appears to be the way of this world.
The powerful gain more and more power
As the weak fall deeper and deeper into despair
In a scratch-my-back, I-will-scratch-yours society.
I wonder, how can all be done within its proper order?
I suppose once placed into a nutshell,
We then can see with clarity.
We often try so hard to lay claim to things
that aren't even ours to claim.
As we begin fumbling, while attempting
to cross the end zone,
We continue to stumble in the dark,
Consistently failing to engage the one true light
that resides forever upon the throne of God.
But fast forward to sound!

I sincerely thank you, Father, for all
of your unconditional love.
Because the truths of everyday life, they play
out on the televisions of this world,
Almost always seen inside as well as throughout
the many outlets of the media.
Help me out, people. Can we become so
blinded that we can't see how our carelessness
is affecting the seeds of tomorrow
As we plant the races of children,
Most being misled by bigotry, biased teachings,
not to mention the hopelessness of fear
Beneath the soul of guilt?
These seeds can only produce a nation in sorrow.
I ask now that all pray
And pray a prayer for open hearts; these minds
need to be filled with love and self-freedom.
We all need light, Father, that life that is our King Jesus.
Grace is giving, yes! But I am wondering:
for how much longer?
Because what man can tell another
the time of our Lord's return,
Or better yet, when to cash out from the table of loss
So that you are sure not to be followed
home by all of your night of regret?
Life's light is a cry for peace and love,
A full and complete turnabout for the troubled in heart.

I trust and believe, my Lord, that your light can see
through our deepest and darkest of moments.
Help us, Father, to make amends with
all we've raged a war against,
Struggling and/or don't seem willing to part with.
Soon, very soon, I can see the place where no
more bloodshed, tears of fear—or anything,
for that matter, to do with sin—will exist.
I believe and shall always follow the light that leads all who
keep your Word into an abode of eternal rest and peace—
My tenth day of this journey.
And may your Word be the guide to a path
of spiritual healing, life's light.

Abba, Father

My heavenly Father, my Father is Lord God, the King of all.
And your love, Abba, truly is the greatest
love I have ever known. Truth!
I have a friend who sticks closer than a brother, my friend.
The light of lights, my Shepherd is the Rose of Sharon.
And Father, it is you who has blessed me with this heart.
So today, inside of life, it really is a must for me;
I have to seek your love out until the end of time!
No matter where this path may lead me, I am yours:
Heart, spirit, this soul, body, and mind.
And so now that you know how I feel
about your love and light,
I continue this journey as an open heart
As well as a clear mind!
Now as I lean back and begin to gaze upon
thy heavenly stars and the moon,
I start to realize that nothing I can ever do will
express the many words I feel deep inside for you,
These emotions that go felt
Day by day within this fragile vessel.

This spirit, Father, in one thought—I
truly do need you, Abba!
Because nothing that is in this world would
exist without your love and light.
Without my Father, how could I continue in this life?
Focusing upon truth, becoming more and
more devoted to fighting the good fight,
On a mission to rise, not to mention, where would I
be able to find reason in this crazy world of ours?
Man made mistakes, yet you continue to bless us all
each and every day with your unfailing grace!
I suppose we only have ourselves to
blame for life's many challenges.
As I sit down with Spirit face to face, I can
really begin analyzing all of this.
Because for every second a new life is born,
somehow in some way, a mother mourns.
And within my final plea of desperation, Abba,
I had cried out for your lightning and
only had heard your thunder,
So I had been spared,
Truly blessed, because instead of receiving the judgement,
I had seen your reign in spirit,
My teacher in self-humility.
I can recall the old man's thoughts as well as remember
how he would often run toward the darkness,
Embracing its pain by way of the world's confusion

As his brother, chaos, continues to corrupt our society.
I feel as though I am being made aware. As I learn, sight
is truly a blessing today by way of your eternal light.
The old man was just so unaware of you, the
purpose of love and the reason behind life,
That beautiful melody we sing as I often
gaze upon each and every sunrise!
Even more so, the old self couldn't grasp my prayer
To become one with the creator of
the heavens and the earth.
God you sent truth, but the enemy plants lies.
But in time, all will soon know which
side it is that they truly do uphold
As creation tries to wait patiently, as your
enemies become your footstool.
A reflection upon the past—
Yes, that old man never did stand a chance
against a love that can never fade.
You redirected my heart, Father,
For every stage had been one well thought out move,
A calculated phase, as each step will
remain, even up to this current day!
Your Word, Abba, is what opened my mind up,
Placing this heart at ease—a soul of one that's anew!
Because who better to give guidance to
the son other than the Father?

A movement of one, a people of earth,
all singing of one love—
A soldier's call for peace
As well as mercy from the Most High.
Just a little more closure to this journeyman's song—
Remember a movement as we all continue to
march on in the name and protection of love,
Abba, Father.

Now I Know

Everything that I had felt,
All I had ever thought I had known—
All had turned out to be a lie. You see, I had
believed the untruths of this world
In what now appears to be all of my life—
That is, until now, this present day in time.
The reality that had been etched into my
mind was truly deception in disguise!
And all of the propaganda within myself
had to now give an account,
Standing before the light of all lights.
I fell; I had fallen hard and fast
To the knees of guilt and shame as well as fear.
But a mercy like no other had shone
its face of grace upon me,
And this is in part my reason for writing this journal:
A calling for the called,
A response unto hope,
A belief within sound,
A drive toward focus!

No matter how high I ever thought that
I was or how low I had ever gone,
Hope was there to bring me right back up.
Regardless of how alone I felt, you comforted me,
This weary soul.
Once, before all of this had started, before
we had ventured out upon this road,
My eyes couldn't conceive truth or its reason
As my heart lay low and confused
Because I never had trusted that a love
could exist as great as this—
Truly unconditional!
Going above and beyond the depths of human regret,
I had to step out in faith and just take a chance,
Never realizing the full extent of my role nor
what this part could've ever commanded!
But here I am,
A tool being used inside of this garden of life.
Hopefully all that's being done is truly pleasing unto thee.
Now through these open eyes, I can see the
morning light shining so brightly
As all of the many flowers in the field rise,
Excited at this sight of new life.
I suppose that one day, all hearts will
embrace their chosen paths—
That is only, Abba Father, if you are willing
to bless all, and allow it to be

Because I believe that all of humanity needs this freedom.

For far too long now, bondage has succeeded.

So now it is the time for the tables to be turned.

In our minds, I know that we can

see the writing on the wall.

But at times, I believe that the struggle is one

Being deeply embedded in our hearts

As mankind screams for a righteous change.

But with that whisper alone, those chains of self-

depravity twist harder upon our wrists

As we all pray for someone to come and bear

this burden of our human shame.

Abba, I now realize that we can't change all in a day.

But you can! Within the love of life, all things are possible.

And that shame, once felt before, is now

exchanged for a crown of righteousness—

That is, only if our heavenly Father is willing.

We all become so much more,

Because in that moment within time and space,

Our entire universe shifts, and the

transposition gives birth on earth,

An entirely new human race,

A people of life, endlessly seeking out wisdom,

longing to speak to you face to face—

That undeniable truth

Behind the wall of self, that selfishness

that is taught to us by this world

As well as that self-disgrace that keeps us sitting
at the table of shame, being lost and afraid.
I pause now in this final moment,
As I can hear my inner man speaking thy message:
"Freedom can be yours if only man would
choose to walk as our Lord did."
Christ Jesus, one who is and was
completely selfless, aware, and free,
Trusting, as all had done before in history,
Before man ran into the camp of darkness,
Indulging self, within the spoils of untruths
And at the same time showering himself in total disbelief—
Thus now I see.
Love is life, and life is love,
As faith remains forever for me true belief.
So now I know I can truly do all things
Because we are so much more than just conquerors.
We are a chosen of a chosen.

♪ DAY THIRTEEN

Sound

Thirty-three—it's a dreamer's reality.

It's light being seen through the darkest of points.

So long live the truth, as our way is

always being formed before us.

Praises to the Most High

Because I can now see forward and beyond

the boundaries of the normal.

My inner thoughts have allowed me to travel even

further than I had ever imagined before this moment

Because I believe that a man in search of answers

can only hope to ask the correct questions.

So then, should they be allowed to build me a house?

Or perhaps you will teach me how to construct

a proper shelter to become my abode

Without the stress of a human doubt.

I take my turn, walking across what appears

to be an enormous tightrope.

And who knows? Perhaps everything is just an illusion,

A giant illustration of any and all things that

we believe to be of the hidden reality,

A message board of some sorts,
A lot of encrypted imagery.
I don't know; maybe it is just the endless
possibilities within this love.
That is what, after all, drives me to the edge
of these so-called safe zones of society
As well as my thinking outside of the box,
So opposite of the way everyday people
may think and view this world.
It is possible that all I can relate to now is the unknown,
The many so-called hopeless and lost souls,
All of whom are looked upon by this world as the underdog,
That special someone who's in search of hope,
A person who's just looking for a chance at a better
situation for themselves as well as their families.
I know that with time, all people will awaken
And realize all of their true potential as human beings,
Tapping into that true power of self
That resides deep down in each heart and soul—
Just another of the many gifts given by our Lord God.
Remember a promise to love forever and ever more.
I can honestly say that I focus every
day on your words, Abba.
Words, like faith, are true belief; these words' vibrations
alone send me to a place and time of self- relief
Into a dream's start, then directly to its end,
And next, all the way back to its peak—

A better focus!

Because I realize believing is conceiving, thus I awaken,

Beginning to shake off all of my past and mistakes.

Yes, because nothing can define me

I won't allow to outline me

Besides with my mind's state.

It is always military grounded,

A foundation of faith,

A reason behind living life now for each and every day.

I allow your poetry to have its way, Abba.

As the sun rises and the moon shines,

I listen to the melody of light.

But regardless of whatever, your love is always on time.

We've begun this journey together,

And no matter what tomorrow may bring

From here on out,

Life will be one lived within the moment,

Because life isn't promised tomorrow.

So why sweat the small stuff

When there's so much of your love and grace in

everything we can see, smell, and even taste?

Truth told, I believe that we are finally

maturing in your light of love.

We're all beginning to rise up to the challenge,

Placing all of our faith into one,

The very same one who had taught us

all to love in the first place,

The light of lights, Rose of Sharon, my heart's echo,
my mission statement, as well as will to carry on,
Now present-day, one with all,
A voice that has learned to share as
well as sing with life's chorus,
Praying that once all is said and done,
Every one of our voices will produce for
you, Abba, a beautiful melody
And a powerful praise—
All in all, a wonderful sound.
I'm just one, a soldier sharing his light
of this journey until the next.
May the love of all loves lead, guide, and
continue to protect all hearts and minds
As we all journey here within space and time—
One light,
One love,
One truth,
One Father, truth,
One sound.
Thirty-three—the light of this soldier's journey!

ABOUT THE AUTHOR

Every since I could remember. Life had its hold on me. I could not understand it, but as time went on, I learned how to grow and embrace that one voice, that had been calling out to me all along. And now I know, I know that today is my time to share with the entire world. My song, this light. My story, being told in a way that only I can share, tell it.

Printed in the United States
By Bookmasters